THE DUMBEST IDEA EVER!

BY
JIMMY GOWNLEY

graphix
AN IMPRINT OF
■SCHOLASTIC

"Cartoonists don't live anywhere. They aren't real people."
— Charles M. Schulz

This book is dedicated to the memory of Tony Graziano (1972–1994).
And to all the Girardville kids . . . past, present, and future.

All rights reserved. Published by Graphix, an imprint of Scholastic Inc., *Publishers since 1920*. SCHOLASTIC, GRAPHIX, and associated logos are trademarks and/or registered trademarks of Scholastic Inc.

Library of Congress Control Number: 2013939128

ISBN 978-0-545-45346-2 (hardcover)
ISBN 978-0-545-45347-9 (paperback)

10 9 8 7 6 5 4 3 2 1   14 15 16 17 18
Printed in China   38

First edition, March 2014
Edited by Adam Rau
Book design by Phil Falco
Creative Director: David Saylor
I hope you're having fun.

SORRY! IS *THIS* ANY BETTER?

GREAT! AFTER ALL, WE NEED TO SEE THE BOY BEHIND THE BOOK.

OH, OKAY.

SO, JIMMY JUST TO DOUBLE CHECK...

THIS COMIC BOOK OF YOURS...YOU WROTE IT, DREW IT, AND PUBLISHED IT YOURSELF?

WELL, MY PARENTS HELPED ME GET IT PRINTED, BUT I DID THE REST MYSELF.

PRETTY IMPRESSIVE.

THANKS.

UMM... I'M *REALLY* NERVOUS.

I'VE NEVER BEEN INTERVIEWED ON *TV* BEFORE.

JUST RELAX AND BE YOURSELF.

FIRST, CAN YOU SPELL YOUR NAME FOR US?

JAY-EYE-EM-EM-WHY -- GEE-OH-DOUBLE YOU- EN- EL- EEE- WHY.

AND THAT'S PRONOUNCED?

GOWN.

LEE.

LIKE "WEDDING GOWN..."

...AND "STAN LEE."

"OKAY, SO JIMMY... AT JUST FIFTEEN YOU'VE WRITTEN AND PUBLISHED YOUR FIRST COMIC BOOK ..."

... NOW THAT COMIC IS GOING INTO ITS SECOND PRINTING, AND YOU'RE ALREADY MAKING ANOTHER ONE.

THAT'S RIGHT.

THAT'S PRETTY CREATIVE FOR SOMEONE YOUR AGE.

SO TELL ME...

...WHERE DO YOU GET YOUR IDEAS?

OH! UMM... WELL...

"...DON'T GO DOWN IN THE MIIIIINE, DAD"

JIMMY! THERE YOU ARE!

IT'S ABOUT TIME YOU GOT HOME. SAY HELLO TO YOUR AUNTS AND UNCLES.

HELLO, AUNTS AND UNCLES.

MERRY CHRISTMAS!

YOU'RE MISSING THE SING-ALONG.

WE JUST FINISHED "DON'T GO DOWN IN THE MINE, DAD."

YEAH, I *HEARD*... THE WHOLE *STREET* HEARD.

Y'KNOW, MOST FAMILIES SING *CHRISTMAS CAROLS*...

NOT SONGS ABOUT 19TH CENTURY MINING DISASTERS.

SO, WHAT WERE YOU DOING OUT SO LATE? ROBBING A *BANK*?

HA-HA

NO!

I WAS JUST DOWN THE STREET LOOKING FOR *MARNIE MARQUARDT*.

THE GIRL FROM THE NEXT BLOCK?

I THOUGHT SHE MOVED AWAY.

SHE DID, BUT HER AUNT SAID SHE WAS GONNA VISIT HER GRANDMA TODAY.

I WENT BY THE HOUSE BUT ALL OF THE LIGHTS WERE OUT.

AWW.., I BET YOU MISS YOUR LITTLE GIRLFRIEND.

SHE WAS **NOT** MY **GIRLFRIEND!**

AND YES.

THE TRUTH IS, GIRARDVILLE IS JUST A SLATE-GRAY SCRAMBLE OF ROW HOMES AND ROCKS PLOPPED IN THE MIDDLE OF PENNSYLVANIA'S COAL REGION.

WELCOME TO
Girardville
ESTABLISHED 1832

IT'S HOME TO SIX CHURCHES...

OPEN

... SEVENTEEN BARS...

... ZERO LIBRARIES...

...AND *ME*.

HEY!

HEY!

12

I'D LIKE TO CONGRATULATE OUR IMMACULATE HEART HAWKS ON THEIR WIN THIS SUNDAY...

...AND MR. GOWNLEY...

...I UNDERSTAND YOU SCORED SIXTEEN POINTS!

EIGHTEEN POINTS, SISTER REBEKAH!

EIGHTEEN POINTS!

CONGRATULATIONS.

THANK YOU, SISTER REBEKAH.

UNFORTUNATELY, I ALSO NEED TO NOTE THAT WE HAVE SIX STUDENTS OUT WITH CHICKEN POX.

I'M GOING TO HAVE TO TAKE A MOMENT TO RETHINK MY LESSON PLAN.

SO, EVERYONE CAN USE THIS PERIOD TO READ INDEPENDENTLY.

17

RRRRIIIIINNG!

YOU... ...YOU WANTED TO SEE ME, SISTER?

YES.

MR. GOWNLEY, AS THE TOP STUDENT IN THIS CLASS, I EXPECT MORE FROM YOU.

TRASH LIKE THIS IS NEVER ACCEPTABLE IN THIS CLASSROOM.

TOMORROW, BRING IN SOMETHING MORE APPROPRIATE FOR SCHOOL.

YES, SISTER.

ACTUALLY, SISTER... I THINK THIS _IS_ APPROPRIATE.

...I THINK IT'S GREAT.

OH, PLEASE! YOU ARE *SUCH A GOOD READER!* WHY WASTE YOUR TIME WITH JUNK?

I KNOW I'M A GOOD READER! HOW DO YOU THINK I **GOT** THAT WAY?

YOU "GOT THAT WAY" BECAUSE OF YOUR *TEACHERS!* SISTER RUTH! MRS. EICHE! MISS KLINGER!

BATMAN!

"BATMAN"?

YEAH! **YOU** KNOW...

...THE **PEOPLE** WHO **WORK** ON **BATMAN!** THE **WRITERS!** **GAH!** YOU **KNOW** WHAT I **MEAN!**

WELL, DON'T GET *ANGRY.*

I'M **NOT ANGRY!**

I'M JUST...

FRUSTRATED!

OKAY. SETTLE DOWN.

I HAVE AN IDEA.

AND MINE SHOULD BE ABOUT THE VALUE OF *COMIC BOOKS* IN EDUCATION.

WAIT! THE WHOLE CLASS HAS TO DO THESE THINGS?

YEAH, SHE'S GONNA ANNOUNCE IT TOMORROW ANYWAY, SO SHE JUST TOLD ME *EARLY.*

THAT *STINKS!* THE CHAMPIONSHIP IS *NEXT FRIDAY.*

WE NEED TO *FOCUS.*

I KNOW, FRANKIE, BUT MY PRESENTATION HAS TO BE *GREAT.*

I WANT HER TO SEE HOW WRONG SHE WAS TO YELL AT ME LIKE THAT.

SHUT UP!

LOOK WHO'S COMING...

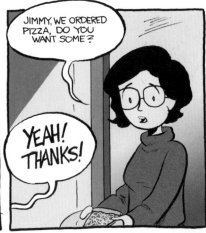

JIMMY, WE ORDERED PIZZA, DO YOU WANT SOME?

YEAH! THANKS!

YOU'RE STILL WORKING ON THAT *PRESENTATION?* YOU'VE BEEN AT IT FOR *DAYS*.

YOU'LL DEFINITELY GET AN *A* WITH ALL OF THE WORK YOU PUT IN.

THIS ISN'T ABOUT THE *GRADE*.

I'M *TRYING* TO PROVE A *POINT*.

=SIGH=

YOU'RE YOUR FATHER ALL OVER AGAIN.

-AHEM-

GRAPHIC LITERATURE... MORE COMMONLY KNOWN BY THE MISLEADING TERM *"COMIC BOOK"...* IS ONE OF AMERICA'S FEW IN... IN... IN*DIG*ENOUS ART FORMS.

IT... UMM..., IT IS A MULTIMILLION-DOLLAR INDUSTRY THAT EMPLOYS SOME OF OUR COUNTRY'S GREATEST WRITERS AND ARTISTS.

COMICS HAVE BEEN USED BY OUR ARMED FORCES TO TRAIN SOLDIERS...

...AND BY TEACHERS TO HELP IMMIGRANT CHILDREN LEARN ENGLISH.

Presentation TODAY!

TODAY I'M GOING TO TALK SPECIFICALLY ABOUT COMICS' POTENTIAL ROLE IN EDUCATION.

BUT FIRST...

...A DRAMATIC READING.

27

THIS IS AWFUL!

I'M THE TEAM'S LEADING SCORER.

I SHOULD BE PLAYING!

YOU'RE SICK! YOU'D INFECT EVERYBODY!

GOOD! I COULD INFECT THE OTHER TEAM AND WATCH THEM SCRATCH THEMSELVES DOWN TO TINY LOSER NUBS.

JUST RELAX AND DRAW. I'M SURE YOUR DAD WILL CALL AGAIN--

RRIIING RRIIING

HELLO?

HELLO, DAD?

UH-HUH!

UH-HUH!

AWESOME!

WE'RE UP EIGHT WITH TWO MINUTES TO GO IN THE FOURTH...

WE CAN'T LOSE.

HEY, MOM... IF I GET THIS *FINISHED*, WILL YOU TAKE IT DOWN TO SCHOOL TOMORROW FOR THE GUYS?

SURE JIMMY...

...BUT MAYBE YOU SHOULD WAIT TO FINISH IT...

Y'KNOW...WHEN YOU KNOW YOU'VE WON.

MOMMM!

YOU'RE *SUCH* A WORRY-WORT!

I JUST DON'T WANT YOU TO BE UPSET IF SOMETHING *BAD* HAPPENS.

BUT IT *IS* NICE TO SEE YOU *HAPPY*.

35

I *GUESS* I AM. THERE'S JUST ONE THING...

...I DIDN'T GET TO BE A PART OF IT.

JIMMY! THAT'S *NOT* *TRUE!* YOU WERE A *BIG* PART OF THE *WHOLE* SEASON!

YEAH, BUT NOT THE *CHAMPIONSHIP!*

CHAMPIONS

HAWK

SO, WHO CARES ABOUT--

RRRIIING

ZIP

DAD? WHAT'S--

WHAT?!

MAN, I NEVER THOUGHT I'D THINK *THAT!*

BUT I'M JUST GLAD TO GET OFF THIS COUCH.

EVEN IF I STILL DON'T FEEL GREAT.

> SIGH <

MAYBE I JUST NEED TO GET BACK INTO A ROUTINE.

MOAN!

A MONTH.

BETWEEN THIS AND CHICKEN POX, IT'LL BE A MONTH OF LYING ON THIS DUMB *COUCH*.

NO FUN. NO FRIENDS. NO SPORTS... *NOTHING!*

AND WHEN I GET BETTER... *THEN* WHAT?

EVERYTHING JUST GOES BACK TO THE WAY IT *WAS?*

THE *SCHOOL*, THE *PRESSURE*, THE *EXPECTATIONS*... IT'S ALL GONNA COME BACK.

NO.

NO. I'M JUST GONNA FORGET IT ALL.

I'M JUST GONNA LIE HERE UNTIL I DIE.

MOAN!

BLOINK!

We need to **TALK**.

is this... it?

is this... my time?

Dude, *GET a GRIP!* You're **NOT** DYING!

You have, like, a **BAD COLD** or something.

Chill out.

IF I'M NOT DYING, WHY ARE **YOU** HERE?

HONestly?

It's the CONSTANT, whining!

I heard **THAT**, and figured someone really *WAS* dying...

..but, I *GET* here...

... and it's just **YOU.**

GEE. SORRY TO DISAPPOINT YOU!

LOOK, you want some **FREE ADVICE?**

You need to **LIGHTEN UP.**

You put too much **PRESSURE** on yourself.

NOT everything has to be so... **GRIM...** y'know?

You're **NOT DYING.** In fact, your whole **LIFE** is ahead of you...

...any life you **WANT.** actually.

All you have to do...

...is **LIVE** it..

46

HONESTLY? I'M GETTING WORRIED. I THINK HE'S TALKING TO HIMSELF.

OKAY. I'LL TELL HIM.

JIMMY, IT'S YOUR COUSIN ANN MARIE. SHE WANTS TO KNOW HOW YOU'RE FEELING.

SIGH WELL, SHE SAID TO TURN ON CHANNEL 4. THERE'S A SHOW ON YOU MIGHT LIKE.

CLICK

Comic books, those brightly colored pamphlets traditionally read by children, half-wits, and the criminally insane, have been getting a makeover lately.

Joining us today to talk about this, let's go with "interesting," art form, is Gene Suzko, owner of GeMa Books... a comic book store located in Wilkes Barre, PA.

Gene, tell me, aren't comic books just dumbed-down fantasies for arrested adolescents afraid to leave their mothers' basements?

Not at all, Steve. In my shop we sell comics and graphic novels on all sorts of topics that appeal to a wide variety of readers.

GOOD MORNING, SISTER. HERE ARE ALL MY ASSIGNMENTS.

MISTER GOWNLEY, NICE TO HAVE YOU BACK.

YOU CAN TAKE YOUR SEAT.

YOU'RE ALIVE... UHH... *AGAIN.*

MOSTLY.

THANKS FOR BRINGING ALL MY ASSIGNMENTS HOME FOR ME, FRANKIE.

SURE! I KNOW HOW IMPORTANT YOUR GRADES ARE TO YOU.

ARE THEY?

UMM... WELL... SPEAKING OF ASSIGNMENTS... WHAT HISTORIC EVENT DID YOU PICK FOR YOUR ESSAY?

WAIT!

WHAT WHAT DID I *PICK* FOR MY *WHAT*?!

THE ESSAY! IT WAS IN THE PACK OF ASSIGNMENTS I BROUGHT TO YOUR HOUSE.

IT'S DUE TODAY. NO EXCEPTIONS.

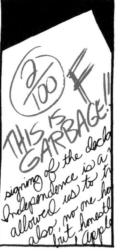

2/100 F

THIS IS GARBAGE!!

signing of the decl...
Independence is a...
allowed us to th...
also, no one ho...
but honestl...
Apple...

COULDN'T AGREE MORE.

HI, MOM. I'M HOME.

JIMMY, HELLO! HOW WAS SCHOOL?

OH, IT WAS OKAY.

I'M GONNA GO START ON MY HOMEWORK, OKAY?

ALL RIGHT, I'LL CALL YOU FOR DINNER. WORK HARD.

DON'T WORRY...

WOW. THAT'S QUITE A HAUL YOU HAVE THERE.

YEP!

I'VE NEVER BEEN TO A COMIC BOOK STORE BEFORE.

I BOUGHT ONE OF EVERYTHING I NEVER HEARD OF.

AND *SOME* LOOK *SUPER* WEIRD.

LIKE, WHAT'S THE DEAL WITH THIS ONE ABOUT THE *DONKEY*?

ACTUALLY, THAT'S AN AARDVARK, AND IT'S ONE OF THE BEST COMICS GOING RIGHT NOW.

BUT YOU CAN ONLY GET IT IN COMIC SHOPS.

IT'S CREATED BY THESE TWO GUYS IN CANADA, AND THERE'S NO BIG COMPANY OR ANYTHING. THEY JUST PUT IT OUT *THEMSELVES*.

AND THEY MAKE *MONEY* THAT WAY?

FLIP

ARE YOU KIDDING? FROM WHAT I'VE SEEN, THEY LIVE LIKE *ROCK STARS*.

HUH.

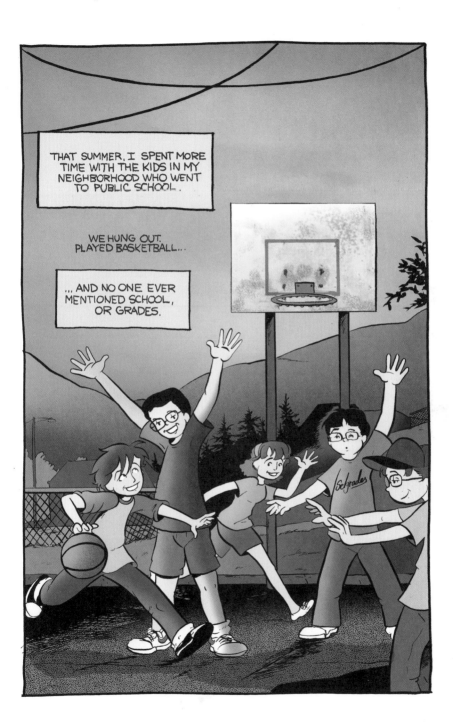

THAT SUMMER, I SPENT MORE TIME WITH THE KIDS IN MY NEIGHBORHOOD WHO WENT TO PUBLIC SCHOOL.

WE HUNG OUT. PLAYED BASKETBALL...

... AND NO ONE EVER MENTIONED SCHOOL, OR GRADES.

HOW DO YOU LIKE BRENNAN SO FAR?

IT IS WHAT IT IS, Y'KNOW?

YEAH.

WHAT DO YOU GUYS THINK ABOUT MR. SHANER FOR GOVERNMENT CLASS?

HE'S *TOUGH*.

YEAH, BUT HE'S FAIR. I DON'T CARE IF YOU'RE TOUGH, AS LONG AS YOU'RE FAIR.

HOW ABOUT SISTER ANN JAMES?

ENGLISH LIT?

I LIKE HER A LOT. SHE'S KIND OF A *HIPPIE*.

YEAH, BUT SOME OF THOSE BOOKS! I MEAN *GREAT EXPECTATIONS? UGH!*

THAT *PIP* CHARACTER NEEDS TO BE *BEATEN* ABOUT THE HEAD AND SHOULDERS.

YEAH, BUT IN CLASS YOU CAN ACTUALLY SAY YOU DON'T LIKE THE BOOK. SHE LETS YOU HAVE AN OPINION, AND THAT'S *REALLY COOL*.

TRUE.

OKAY. NO ONE'S MENTIONED THE OBVIOUS...

...ALGEBRA ONE WITH...

...SISTER REGINA ALMA.

BRRRRR... THE VERY *NAME* SENDS CHILLS DOWN MY *SPINE!*

I HEARD SHE MADE A GIRL *PEE HERSELF.*

NO WAY!

DUDE, I *SWEAR.*

THE GIRL WAS LATE, AND *REGINA ALMA* FREAKED OUT ON HER.

SO THE KID *SPRUNG A LEAK* RIGHT THERE IN *CLASS.*

THAT'S AWFUL!

LIKE HER CLASS ISN'T HARD ENOUGH WITHOUT HER COMPROMISING YOUR *BLADDER CONTROL.*

70

YEAH, THE CLASS IS A *NIGHTMARE*.

LAST NIGHT'S HOMEWORK WAS *KILLER*.

WE HAD *HOMEWORK*?

UHH... YEAH...

LIKE *TEN* PROBLEMS.

SHOOT! I WASN'T PAYING *ATTENTION*.

DUDE, SHE IS GONNA *LOSE* IT.

HOPE YOU HAVE A PAIR OF *DIAPERS*.

SHUT UP! IT'S NOT TILL NEXT PERIOD. I MIGHT HAVE TIME TO—

RRRIIINNG

LOOK...

...MAYBE SHE WON'T CALL ON YOU.

yeah... maybe.

WHAT'S *WRONG?* I'M *DROWNING!* I'M UNHAPPY ALL THE TIME. IT'S NOT YOUR FAULT, AND THERE'S NOTHING YOU CAN DO...

MAYBE THERE'S NOTHING ANYONE CAN DO.

BUT I'M SCARED. I FEEL LIKE I'M LOST, AND I'LL NEVER FIND MY WAY HOME AGAIN.

I'M **FINE!**

YOU WORRY TOO MUCH. SO, I'M HAVING SOME ISSUES AT SCHOOL.

IT'LL WORK OUT IN THE END.

NOW LOOK... TONIGHT WE HAVE TO DECORATE THE GYM FOR BRENNAN DAY.

IT'S A WHOLE SCHOOL PRIDE THING.

AND IT'S ACTUALLY KINDA *FUN.*

BECAUSE THEY'RE THE *FIRST*, AND HAVE THE BEST *SECRET ORIGINS*, Y'KNOW?

I TOTALLY *DON'T* KNOW.

SURE YOU DO! BATMAN'S PARENTS ARE KILLED, SO HE TRAINS HIMSELF TO FIGHT *CRIME*. SUPERMAN'S WHOLE PLANET GETS BLOWN UP AND HE'S SENT TO EARTH TO USE HIS POWERS TO *HELP* PEOPLE.

GEEZ! THAT'S PRETTY *DARK*. DOESN'T ANYONE BECOME A SUPERHERO BY GOING TO A *GOOD COLLEGE?*

NOT THAT I'M AWARE OF, NO.

IT USUALLY HAS TO BE SOMETHING TRAUMATIC. SOMETHING THAT'S BAD AT *FIRST*, BUT THAT MAKES THE HERO BECOME WHAT HE'S SUPPOSED TO BECOME.

YEAH? SO DO YOU HAVE A SECRET ORIGIN, *CARTOON BOY?*

INTERESTING.

YES, *TONY?*

THAT'S NOT EXACTLY WHAT I *MEAN.*

IT'S LIKE... Y'KNOW WHEN YOU'RE WATCHING A *HORROR MOVIE,* AND SOME GUY GOES "I FEEL LIKE I COULD LIVE *FOREVER."*

WELL, YOU *KNOW* THAT GUY'S NOT GONNA MAKE IT THROUGH THE WHOLE MOVIE! AND THAT STUFF RUINS THE WHOLE STORY FOR ME.

JIMMY, YOU HAVE A *COMMENT?*

I JUST THINK THAT SOMETIMES THE WRITER HAS TO USE THOSE *TRICKS* OR WHATEVER, SO THAT PEOPLE CAN UNDERSTAND WHAT HE'S TRYING TO SAY...

".. AND EVEN IF IT'S NOT JUST LIKE *REAL LIFE--*

YOU'RE ALL *MISSING* the *POINT!*

MISTER McCONNELL, INTERRUPTING ISN'T--

IT DOESN'T MATTER ABOUT FORESHADOWING. THE *POINT* IS THAT THE MAIN CHARACTER IS AN *IDIOT.*

HE SPENDS THE FIRST PART OF THE STORY BEING ALL ARROGANT 'CUZ THINGS ARE GOING HIS WAY, BUT WHEN THINGS GET TOUGH, HE *FALLS* APART.

OKAY.

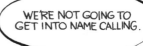

DOES A CHARACTER LIKE THAT RING TRUE TO US AS READERS?

IT DOES TO ME, I KNOW PEOPLE LIKE THAT. THERE ARE PEOPLE LIKE THAT IN THIS ROOM.

WE'RE NOT GOING TO GET INTO NAME CALLING.

I'M NOT CALLING ANYONE *NAMES.*

BUT I KNOW PEOPLE WHO WERE HOT STUFF BEFORE HIGH SCHOOL WHO JUST CAN'T HACK IT NOW.

86

GEEZ! WHAT WAS *THAT* ALL ABOUT?

FRANKIE, I SWEAR I HAVE *NO IDEA.*

WERE YOU GUYS ARGUING BEFORE, OR SOMETHING?

NO. I NEVER EVEN *TALK* TO THE JERK.

SO YOU DON'T KNOW WHY HE WENT *OFF* ON YOU?

NO.

SO THE WHOLE THING CAME OUT OF <u>NOWHERE?</u>

YES!

REAL LIFE *DOESN'T* HAVE *FORESHADOWING.*

SEE? I WAS RIGHT.

89

YAWN!

= CLICK

"THEY JUST PUT IT OUT *THEMSELVES*."

"FROM WHAT I'VE SEEN, THEY LIVE LIKE *ROCK STARS*."

FLIP FLIP

" SO, DO YOU HAVE A SECRET ORIGIN? ")

CCCKAYZ

OH!

AND HE CAN SHOOT THESE, LIKE, FIREBOLTS OUT OF THESE *THINGIES* ON HIS *WRISTS.*

PEWW!
PEWW!
PEWW!

UH-HUH... SO, AM I SUPPOSED TO *READ* THIS, OR ARE YOU JUST GONNA *ACT* IT OUT FOR ME?

OH, RIGHT! HA! IT'S IN MY *LOCKER*.

SO, WHY DO YOU WANT ME TO *READ* IT SO BAD?

WELL... GIRLS LIKE YOU, RIGHT?

IF YOU *SAY* SO...

SO, IF *GIRLS* LIKE *YOU,* AND *YOU* LIKE MY *COMIC BOOK*...

THEN, BY THE *TRANSITIVE PROPERTY,* IPSO FACTO, *GIRLS*...

... WILL LIKE *ME.*

WAIT!
WAIT!
WAIT!

MY NAME'S NOT ELLEN *DOLAN*! IT'S ELLEN *TOOLE*!

SMACK!

IT *IS*? THEN *WHY* DID I THINK...

...OH! *I* KNOW!

ELLEN *DOLAN* IS THE *SPIRIT's* GIRLFRIEND!

WHAT TH--?!

WHO THE HECK IS "The *SPIRIT*"?

HE'S, LIKE, THIS *CRIME FIGHTER* FROM THIS OLD COMIC BOOK. IT'S A *CLASSIC*!

ELLEN DOLAN IS HIS *GIRLFRIEND*, AND SHE'S REALLY COOL! SO... UMM...

...THINKING THAT WAS *YOUR* NAME WAS, LIKE, A... A... *COMPLIMENT!*

JIMMY?

YEAH?

SHUT UP.

RRRIIIIINNG

ALL RIGHT, WELL, I HAVE TO RUN TO GET TO SPANISH CLASS.

UNLIKE YOU SLACKERS...

... ELLEN *TOOLE* DOESN'T GET TARDY SLIPS!

BYEEE!

LATER.

SEE YA!

YOU DO REALIZE THAT SHE LIKES YOU, RIGHT?

WHAT?

NAH... YOU'RE CRAZY!

JIMMY?

YEAH?

SHUT UP.

TONY! HEY, TONY!

HEY!

OH, HEY MAN!

DON'T GIVE ME ANY "HEY, MAN" GARBAGE.

YOU'RE AVOIDING ME.

WHAT?

NO, I'M NOT!

I'VE JUST BEEN BUSY.

OH RIGHT... "BUSY."

I ASK YOU FOR ONE FAVOR!

TO READ MY COMIC BOOK!

AND YOU CAN'T EVEN BE BOTHERED!

103

OKAY. FIRST, IT'S *SUPER* NERDY.

I MEAN, WHO WANTS TO READ ABOUT *EVIL JEWELRY?*

UMMM... HELLOoooo!

EVER HEAR OF *THE LORD OF THE RINGS*?

=SIGH=

HOW CAN I *PUT* THIS?

AH!

=SNAP=

YOU KNOW THOSE GIRLS...DAWN BRENNAN AND TAMMY MEADE?

THE CUTE PUBLIC SCHOOL GIRLS?

RIGHT.

WOULD *THEY* READ ABOUT EVIL SPACE JEWELRY?

OKAY, I SEE YOUR POINT.

IT'S A *NIGHTMARE!*

WHAT IS? YOUR COMIC BOOK?

YEAH. I'VE BEEN STUCK FOR WEEKS.

SO GO BACK TO YOUR *STAR LORD* IDEA IF THIS ISN'T WORKING.

NAH. THAT WAS STUPID. I JUST TOOK *STAR WARS* AND *THE LORD OF THE RINGS* AND SMOOSHED 'EM TOGETHER.

YEAH?

THAT SOUNDS PRETTY COOL.

TRUST ME, IT *WASN'T...*

THANKS FOR COMING, I WASN'T SURE YOU WOULD.

ELLEN! ARE YOU KIDDING? I WAS PSYCHED TO BE INVITED!

REALLY? YOU LOOK SORTA *TIRED*.

YEAH. I WAS KINDA UP ALL NIGHT.

YOU *WERE*? WHAT WERE YOU *DOING*?

DRAWING A COMIC BOOK.

YOU'RE KIDDING, RIGHT?

NO, I'M NOT KIDDING!

WHY WOULD I BE KIDDING!?

RIGHT! YOU WOULDN'T BE! UMM... IT SOUNDS *REALLY COOL*!

UH-*HUH*...SURE

OH... THAT'S OKAY. I HAD A GREAT TIME ANYWAY.

ME TOO.

SO, MAYBE WE CAN DO IT AGAIN SOME OTHER TIME.

YEAH...

... SOME OTHER TIME.

SO, ARE YOU FINISHED, YET?

NO. IT'S TAKING A LOT LONGER THAN I THOUGHT.

I WORKED ON IT ALL SUMMER BUT I STILL HAVE A BUNCH LEFT.

PLUS, I'M NEVER HAPPY WHEN I FINISH A PAGE. IT NEVER LOOKS LIKE IT DOES IN MY *HEAD*.

WELL, ARE THEY GETTING BETTER AS YOU GO ALONG?

ACTUALLY, I DON'T THINK SO.

AND SOMETIMES, THE HARDER I TRY, THE WORSE IT COMES OUT.

SOUNDS LIKE A LOT OF WORK FOR SUMMER VACATION. YOU MUST BE GETTING *SICK* OF IT.

I'M *NOT*, THOUGH.

I KNOW IT'S HARD WORK AND ALL, AND I'M NOT EVEN SURE IF I'M ANY *GOOD* AT IT...

...BUT, I *LOVE* IT.

IT'S KINDA HARD TO *EXPLAIN*...

...BUT, I THINK IT MIGHT BE MY *THING*, Y'KNOW?

130

MOAN!

ARE YOU JUST GONNA LIE THERE, MOANING ALL NIGHT?

MOAN!

>SIGH< WELL, KNOCK IT OFF. I HAVE SOMETHING TO SHOW YOU.

WHAT DID YOU DO?

I TOOK ONE OF THE BOOKS APART.

I THOUGHT MAYBE WE COULD REARRANGE THE PAGES, AND PUT IT BACK TOGETHER.

CAN WE?

NO.

MOAN!

BUT WAIT... I NOTICED SOMETHING ELSE.

HARD? THE WHOLE THING WAS HARD! WRITING AND DRAWING IT WAS HARD! QUITING IS STUPID!

MY **FIRST SALE!**

IT *FEELS...*

...WEIRD!

WELL, GET USED TO IT. I'M SURE IT'S THE FIRST OF MANY.

AND *HEY,* YOU CAN USE THE MONEY FOR THE *MOVIE* TONIGHT! PERFECT TIMING!

♪ SEE YOU THEN, OKAY? ♪

YEP! SEE YA THEN!

SO... ANOTHER "NOT-A-DATE" DATE?

YEAH. I THINK THIS IS NUMBER FOUR.

WILL YOU JUST ASK HER TO BE YOUR *GIRLFRIEND* ALREADY?

THIS IS GETTING OLD!

LOOK, I PROMISE I HAVE EVERY INTENTION OF ASKING HER *TONIGHT!*

I'M **DETERMINED!**

I'M **CONFIDENT!**

143

HAVE YOU EVER NOTICED HOW THERE ARE ONLY, LIKE, *FOUR DIFFERENT* MCNUGGET SHAPES?

I *KNOW!* AND NONE OF THEM ARE SUPER APPETIZING!

THIS ONE LOOKS LIKE A *HUMAN KIDNEY!*

EEEEW! GROSS!

AND CHECK *THIS* OUT...

TWO REGULAR NUGGETS FUSED INTO ONE *GIGANTIC MEGA-NUGGET.*

THAT IS COMPLETELY *DISGUSTING.*

DISGUSTING? I THINK IT'S *ROMANTIC.*

OH, YOU DO, HUH?

145

WILL YOU BE MY GIRLFRIEND?

YES!

YOU WILL?!

ABSOLUTELY!

WOW.

MAY I ASK WHY?

JIMMY, YOU DON'T *SERIOUSLY* WANT TO SIT AND WATCH *GANGSTER DAYS*, DO YOU?

NOPE.

oooKAY...

...WELL, THEN WHY...!?

·OH!·

Umm... ON **SECOND** THOUGHT...

THIRD?

UH-HUH. I NEVER REALLY TOLD ANYONE, BUT I MADE A COMIC WHEN I WAS A *LITTLE KID.*

ACTUALLY, I ALMOST FORGOT ABOUT IT.

I MADE IT AS A *PRESENT* FOR *MARNIE MARQUARDT.*

HUH?

WHAT'S A "MARNIE MARQUARDT"?

OH, THAT'S *RIGHT!*

YOU NEVER *MET* HER.

Marnie Marquardt

WAS THE TOMBOY WHO LIVED UP THE STREET FROM ME.

SHE WAS COOL. SHE WAS FUNNY. AND WE LIKED THE SAME THINGS. SHE EVEN LIKED **STAR WARS** ENOUGH TO FORM A JEDI KNIGHT CLUB WITH ME, AND WE DEFENDED THE STREETS OF GIRARDVILLE FROM EVIL SITH LORDS...

TASTE JEDI JUSTICE!

"JEDI" ME!

"JEDI" MARNIE!

YAGH!

SUSPECTED "SITH"!

...WHICH, TO THE UNTRAINED EYE, MAY HAVE APPEARED LIKE TWO WEIRD KIDS IN BATHROBES SWINGING WIFFLE BALL BATS.

EAT "the FORCE," YOU SITH DIRTBAG!

ACTUAL ME!

WHAT IS WRONG WITH YOU WEIRDOS?!

ACTUAL MARNIE!

RANDOM NEIGHBORHOOD IDIOT!

THE CLUB ONLY LASTED AN AFTERNOON, BUT FOR FOUR YEARS WE WERE INSEPARABLE.

MAN, I CAN'T BELIEVE SUMMER IS HALF OVER. WE'LL BE BACK IN SCHOOL SOON.

YEAH. I GUESS SO.

I WONDER IF OUR LUNCH TABLES WILL BE CLOSE TO EACH OTHER? OR IF WE'LL HAVE RECESS TOGETHER? AND DO YOU THINK—

LOOK! I DON'T KNOW, ALL RIGHT?!

WILL YOU JUST SHUT UP ABOUT IT?!

OKAY! OKAY!

GEEZ, WHAT'S YOUR PROBLEM?

I'M SORRY, I.. LOOK, CAN WE JUST NOT TALK ABOUT SCHOOL?

OH.. UH.. YEAH...

...YEAH, SURE!

HOW IS MARNIE DOING?

OKAY, I GUESS, BUT KINDA GRUMPY.

I GUESS SHE HAS A LOT ON HER MIND.

SHE DOES? WHY?

WELL, GETTING READY TO MOVE AWAY AND ALL...

MOVE AWAY?!

SHE...

...SHE DIDN'T TELL YOU?

EXCUSE ME.

I DON'T FEEL VERY GOOD.

BUT LATER...

...ALONE IN MY SPIDER-MAN UNDEROOS...

...I CONTEMPLATED A MARNIELESS EXISTENCE.

SO, SHE NEVER EVEN GOT TO *SEE* IT?

NO.

THAT'S SO *SAD.*

YOU LIKED HER A LOT, DIDN'T YOU?

YEAH. SHE WAS ONE OF MY BEST FRIENDS. I *STILL* MISS HER.

I CAN TELL.

JIMMY? I HAVE A CONFESSION.

WHAT'S THAT?

I *HATE* MARNIE MARQUARDT.

IT'S SO COOL THAT YOUR MOM OWNS A VIDEO STORE.

OH, WE ARE LIVING THE DREAM, ALL RIGHT.

ANYWAY, MY MOM AND SISTER HAVE A SURPRISE FOR YOU.

REALLY? WHAT--

WHoA!

Mister Mike's Video

TA-DA!

ON SALE!

WE GOT A BUNCH OF COPIES FROM YOUR MOM THAT WE WANT YOU TO SIGN, AND TRACY HAS ANOTHER SURPRISE FOR YOU.

TRACY! SHOW HIM.

I MADE 'EM IN SHOP CLASS.

WOW!

I CAN MAKE MORE, TOO. I FIGURED WE COULD SELL THEM.

OH, MY GOD! I HAVE MERCH! THANK YOU SO MUCH!

I DID, AND I LIKED IT A LOT.

I THOUGHT IT WAS VERY FUNNY.

THANKS! I WORKED REALLY HARD ON IT.

WELL, IT SHOWS.

THAT KID... STEVE... THE ONE YOU JUST GAVE THE BOOK TO.

YOU KNOW HIS FAMILY DOESN'T HAVE TWO NICKELS TO RUB TOGETHER, RIGHT?

YEAH.

YEAH, I KNOW.

WELL, IT'S GOOD TO KNOW THAT IN TWENTY YEARS OF TEACHING, I TAUGHT ONE OR TWO NICE KIDS.

TRY NOT TO BECOME A JERK.

169

I WONDER WHAT MADE HIM SAY *THAT?*

ERT!

CONGRATULATIONS JIMMY...

Shades of Gray
COMICS AND STORIES

OUR CELEBRITY!!!

WHEN DID **THIS** GO UP?

JUST NOW. THE GUIDANCE COUNSELOR DID IT.

YES, MISTER GOWNLEY, YOU'VE BEEN MAKING QUITE THE IMPRESSION LATELY.

OH!

UMM... *HI*, SISTER REGINA ALMA!

YES! I...I GUESS SO!

WELL, YOU DO HAVE A TALENT... SUCH AS IT IS... AND YOU FOUND A WAY TO USE IT.

THAT'S MORE THAN MOST PEOPLE CAN SAY.

NICE JOB.

THANK YOU, SISTER!

WHAT IS HAPPENING?

OH! UMM... WELL...

THAT'S A GOOD QUESTION.

I DON'T KNOW REALLY.

It's just stuff that I notice, or stuff that I think about sometimes. Stuff that I find funny or interesting.

DO YOU FEEL THAT YOUR WORK HAS A MESSAGE?

Well, I guess...hmmm...I guess if people read the book and think about the things the characters go through...

...maybe they'd realize that the things kids think about or experience are serious, y'know? Or at least they are to kids...

"I THINK SOMETIMES ADULTS FORGET THAT."

SAW YOU ON **TV**!

YOU DID **GREAT**!

WERE YOU NERVOUS?

I BOUGHT A COMIC FOR MY NIECE.

GREAT TO SEE A LOCAL KID MAKE GOOD.

YOU'RE SO **TALENTED**.

NOW, ARE YA GONNA WIN THIS GAME TONIGHT?

WELL, IT DOES FEEL GOOD HAVING THE HOME COURT ADVANTAGE.

HEY THERE **BIG STAR**!'

HA! WELL, YOU KNOW HOW IT IS.

YOU LOOKED VERY CUTE ON T.V. I'M PROUD OF YOU.

THANKS!

NOW, IF YOU'LL EXCUSE ME, WE HAVE A GAME SO I NEED TO GO AND EXCEL AT YET ANOTHER THING.

-SIGH-

THEY'VE CREATED A **MONSTER**.

WELL, CHECK IT OUT! A HUGE ARTICLE ABOUT YOURS TRULY.

WOW.

COOL.

EVEN...ALD

TE N CARTOONIST

YEAH, I GUESS THEY WANTED TO BOOST THE OL' CIRCULATION, SO THEY FEATURED *ME*.

HEH HEH

HEY, JIMMY... IS THAT YOU IN THE PAPER?

DUH, EINSTEIN.

IT'S AN ARTICLE ABOUT MY COMIC.

OH YEAH. I READ YOUR BOOK, BUT I DIDN'T REALLY GET IT.

I'M NOT SURPRISED. YOU'RE KIND OF AN IDIOT.

DROP DEAD, JERK!

BACK AT YA, LOSER!

SO! HOW ABOUT THAT GAME ON FRIDAY? WAS THAT SOMETHING OR *WHAT?*

WE LOST.

BADLY.

MAN! WHY IS EVERYONE SO *HUNG-UP* ON THAT?

SO, MY SECOND COMIC WILL BE COMING OUT SOON.

DO YOU THINK I SHOULD START CHARGING FOR *AUTOGRAPHS?*

OH, DON'T WORRY... I'LL GIVE TEAMMATES A *DISCOUNT.*

WHAT? THE *NEW YORK* TRIP? WHO *CARES?* THEY DO IT *EVERY YEAR.*

YEAH... BUT *THIS* YEAR, *WE* ARE GOING *TOGETHER.*

ELLEN, C'MON! IT'S JUST *WAY* TOO *EXPENSIVE.* I'D HAVE TO PAY FOR THE *BUS,* AND BUY A TICKET FOR THE *SHOW...*

...*PLUS,* THERE ARE ALL OF THE *MEALS* AND STUFF... IT'S JUST *TOO* MUCH.

NOT A *PROBLEM.*

MY DAD IS PAYING FOR THE *WHOLE TRIP* FOR ME AND A FRIEND OF MY *CHOOSING...*

...AND I'M CHOOSING *YOU,* FRIEND OF *MINE.*

SPRING TRI[P]
[NE]W YOR[K]
[CI]TY!
April 14
See a
[s]how!

SERIOUSLY?

SERIOUSLY.

WOW!

BEEP! BEEP! BEEP!

5:00 AM

SLEEPY, HUH?

Y'KNOW, I GET UP EVERY DAY AT THIS TIME.

WELL, THAT SUCKS.

AHH...

YA GET USED TO IT.

189

VASE OF IRISES BY VINCENT VAN GOGH.

IT'S PRETTY.

UH-HUH.

BUT I'VE NEVER BEEN A BIG FAN OF HIS, Y'KNOW?

YOU CAN SEE EVERY BRUSH-STROKE.

AND THE WHOLE EAR THING? I MEAN GROSS!

HE WAS JUST SOME GUY, BUT HE DID THIS!

WHAT DO YOU... UHH...JIMMY?

IT STILL LOOKS WET!

IT WAS AMAZING!

THE SHOW! THE CITY! EVERYTHING!

AND WE WENT TO THIS MUSEUM, Y'KNOW? THE BIG ONE? AND WE SAW ALL THESE PAINTINGS...

REAL PICASSOS! REAL MONETS!

IT WAS... I MEAN... I'VE SEEN PICTURES, BUT YOU CAN'T UNDERSTAND UNTIL YOU JUST CAN'T!

I...

ARE YOU OKAY? YOU'RE GETTING VERY WORKED UP.

SORRY, I... I'M JUST TIRED!

I THINK I'M JUST GONNA GO UP TO MY ROOM.

I KINDA NEED TO BE ALONE...

CUTE DATE!

WHY IS SHE WITH YOU?

WELL, THERE'S NO ACCOUNTING FOR *TASTE.*

HEY, LISTEN... I JUST WANTED TO SAY THAT I WAS SORRY.

HUH?

FOR *WHAT?*

FOR CANCELING YOUR BIG DAY. I SHOULDN'T HAVE DONE THAT.

...AND DOWN THERE WAS WHERE WE PLAYED BASKETBALL, AND RIGHT UP THERE WAS WHERE MARNIE LIVED.

UGH! YOU MEAN YOUR LITTLE *GIRLFRIEND?*

SHE WAS *NOT* MY *GIRLFRIEND!*

WE WERE LITTLE KIDS!

YEAH YEAH YEAH.

THE AMUSEMENT PARK WAS FUN TODAY, WASN'T IT?

IT WAS! IT WAS **ALL** FUN.

IT WAS THE *PERFECT* PROM WEEKEND.

BUT IT'S LATE.

AND IT'S PRETTY SWEET AND SENTIMENTAL. I DIDN'T KNOW YOU FELT THAT WAY ABOUT GOOD OL' GIRARDVILLE.

I DIDN'T, Y'KNOW? BUT NEW YORK CHANGED THINGS FOR ME.

IT *DID*?

YEAH. SEEING ALL OF THOSE ARTISTS, THOSE *GENIUSES*, I REALIZED SOMETHING...

...I HAVE **NO TALENT** WHATSOEVER!

JIMMY! THAT'S **NOT** TRUE!

NO, IT IS! AND I'M OKAY WITH IT!

LOOK, IF I WAS A KID IN NEW YORK, OR L.A., NO ONE WOULD HAVE CARED ABOUT MY DUMB COMICS.

I WOULDN'T HAVE BEEN ON TV, OR IN THE PAPER.

JIFFY MART

THE ONLY REASON, THOSE BOOKS WERE SPECIAL, WAS BECAUSE EVERYONE *BELIEVED* THEY WERE SPECIAL.

BELIEVED *I* WAS SPECIAL.

OKAY, OKAY. I PROMISE...

...YOU WEIRDO.

ANYTHING ELSE?

WELL...

...THERE *IS* JUST ONE...

...LITTLE...

...THING.

HAVE A PEPPERMINT.

UMM...

...OKAY, I...

WHY *MISS TOOLE!* I AM *SHOCKED! SHOCKED!* IS THIS ANY WAY FOR A *PROPER YOUNG LADY* TO *BEHAVE?!*

SIGH

JIMMY?

YEAH?

214

SO, WHAT HAPPENED?

I DON'T KNOW.

HOW CAN YOU NOT KNOW?

I DON'T WANT TO TALK ABOUT IT.

WAIT. YOU DON'T WANT TO TALK ABOUT HOW YOU DON'T KNOW WHAT HAPPENED, OR YOU DO KNOW WHAT HAPPENED, AND YOU DON'T WANT TO TALK ABOUT *THAT*?

WE...

WE STARTED ARGUING A LITTLE... THEN WE STARTED ARGUING A *LOT*.

THEN WE HAD ONE *BIG* ARGUMENT.

AND THAT WAS IT?

THAT WAS IT.

LOOK, FORGET ABOUT THAT. THERE ARE LOTS OF GIRLS.

JUST WORK ON GETTING YOUR NEXT COMIC DONE.

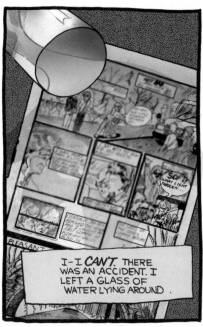

I-I *CAN'T.* THERE WAS AN ACCIDENT. I LEFT A GLASS OF WATER LYING AROUND.

IT GOT SPILLED ON THE PAGES. IT RUINED EVERY SINGLE ONE.

ALL THAT WORK, AND IT JUST WASHED AWAY LIKE IT NEVER HAPPENED AT ALL.

YOU'VE BEEN SITTING THERE FOR HOURS, BUT NOT REALLY DRAWING...

...AND YOU'VE BEEN SO MOPEY.

DO YOU WANT TO TALK ABOUT SOMETHING?

NO. IT'S OKAY... I'M FINE.

I THINK I'LL JUST TAKE A WALK AND CLEAR MY HEAD.

WELL, HOW CAN I HELP?

I NEED TO KNOW ALL OF IT.

HOW CAN I GET A COMIC INTO REAL COMIC STORES?

HOW DO I EXHIBIT AT CONVENTIONS?

HOW DO I GET REVIEWS?

I NEED TO KNOW IT ALL, BECAUSE I'M GONNA HAVE A *REAL* COMIC BOOK SERIES AS SOON AS *POSSIBLE.*

WELL, I GOTTA GIVE IT TO YOU... YOU SURE ARE PERSISTENT.

ACTUALLY, I'M JUST TOO DUMB TO QUIT.

SO, DO YOU HAVE AN IDEA FOR THIS COMIC BOOK?

I SURE DO.

GREAT! I'VE ALWAYS WONDERED WHERE YOU CREATIVE TYPES GET YOUR IDEAS...

...BUT I GUESS IT'S JUST A MYSTERY.

NOPE.

I KNOW EXACTLY WHERE MY IDEA CAME FROM...

"...IT'S GONNA BE OKAY."

OKAY. HERE WE GO...

I STILL HAVE MY DESK...

...SOME PENCILS...

...SOME PAPER...

MY HEART'S BROKEN, ALL OF MY PREVIOUS WORK IS PRETTY MUCH USELESS...

...AND I'M YEARS AWAY FROM A GOAL THAT MIGHT NOT EVEN BE ATTAINABLE.

FEELS GOOD HAVING THE HOME COURT ADVANTAGE.

ANYWAY, I CAN'T THINK ABOUT ALL OF THAT...

...ALL I CAN FOCUS ON IS WHAT IS HERE AND NOW...

...AND RIGHT *HERE*...

...RIGHT *NOW*...

AUTHOR'S NOTE

The Dumbest Idea Ever! is my story. And it's a story about beginnings. This book takes place primarily between the years 1985–1990, and it's set in Girardville, a small, economically struggling coal-mining town in northeastern Pennsylvania. My hometown can be pretty rough, but it was also a fun place to grow up.

I'm the only child of a former coal miner and a homemaker. By the time I was three, my mom had taught me to read using homemade flash cards and by reading me Charles Schulz's comic strip, *Peanuts*. I loved *Peanuts*, and I would sometimes take Mom's flash cards and arrange them to make my own comic strip stories. This, along with the fact that my dad grew up reading comic books, cemented my interest in comics.

My first attempt at writing a comic book was a mash-up of *Star Wars* and *Lord of the Rings*. It took about a month to produce three pages, but it was worth it because I was pretty sure they were genius. Before I unleashed my story on the world (or finished it for that matter), I showed it to my friend Tony to get his opinion. He politely informed me that my story was horrible and that no one on earth would ever read it. Then he made the statement that would change my life: "Why don't you write a comic book about us?"

At the time, I thought this was a really dumb idea. But not having any better ones, I did it anyway.

And I'm glad I did — because eventually I discovered the power of Tony's advice. When I did write comic books about us — about real life — I could reach people who might not otherwise read comics.

So I studied, I learned, and by the time I was twenty I was able to self-publish a new version of my *Shades of Gray* comic, which reached a nationwide audience through comic book stores. I put one in an envelope and sent it to Tony, who was then at Johns Hopkins medical center battling leukemia.

Not long after, I got a call from Ellen Toole. Tony had passed away. That comic book turned out to be the last present I was able to give him.

Which still makes me sad. I think about him every day.

But this is a story about beginnings.

Now I'm a professional cartoonist. My Amelia Rules! series has won awards, been translated into other languages, and even became a *New York Times* bestseller. As part of my job, I go around the country speaking at schools and libraries and conventions, and I tell kids the story of how Tony suggested I write about us. I even told it to Ellen's daughter at an assembly at her school. And every time I'm getting ready to leave an event, I see kids with pens and paper, scribbling furiously, trying to capture their own visions, putting their own stories down on paper.

And I watch the story begin again.

ABOUT THE AUTHOR

Jimmy Gownley began writing and drawing comics at age fifteen and has been nominated for the Eisner Award eleven times. In 2001, his hit series Amelia Rules! was released amid a flurry of rave reviews. He cofounded the organization Kids Love Comics, which works to promote comic books and graphic novels as valuable tools for literacy and education in schools, libraries, and at home. Jimmy lives in Harrisburg, Pennsylvania.